SUPERMOTO

nowwhat.com

BY RAY McCLELLAN

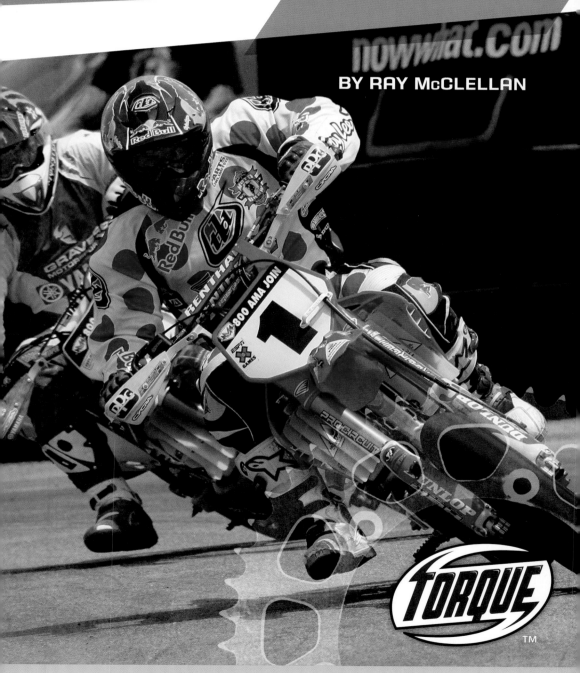

BELLWETHER MEDIA · MINNEAPOLIS, MN

Are you ready to take it to the extreme?
Torque books thrust you into the action-packed world
of sports, vehicles, and adventure. These books may
include dirt, smoke, fire, and dangerous stunts.
WARNING: Read at your own risk.

This edition first published in 2008 by Bellwether Media.

No part of this publication may be reproduced in whole or in part without written permission of the publisher. For information regarding permission, write to Bellwether Media Inc., Attention: Permissions Department, Post Office Box 19349, Minneapolis, MN 55419.

Library of Congress Cataloging-in-Publication Data
McClellan, Ray.
  Supermoto / by Ray McClellan.
    p. cm. — (Torque: action sports)
  Summary: "Amazing photography accompanies engaging information about Supermoto. The combination of high-interest subject matter and light text is intended for students in grades 3 through 7"—Provided by publisher.
  Includes bibliographical references and index.
  ISBN-13: 978-1-60014-144-7 (hardcover : alk. paper)
  ISBN-10: 1-60014-144-7 (hardcover : alk. paper)
  1. Supermoto—Juvenile literature. I. Title.

  GV1060.1457.M33 2008
  796.7'56—dc22   2007040558

Schol. 8/09

CONTENTS

WHAT IS SUPERMOTO?

Motorcycle **road races** thrill fans with high speeds and bursts of acceleration. **Motocross** races offer the excitement of high-flying jumps and skidding turns on dirt. Supermoto is the best of both worlds.

Supermoto racing was started in 1979 by the ABC television network. They wanted to find the best all-round motorcycle racer in the world.

They created "superbike" races that combined paved-road racing with the dirt riding and jumps of motocross. The sport became known as supermoto.

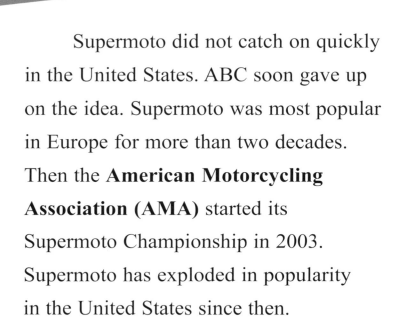

Supermoto did not catch on quickly in the United States. ABC soon gave up on the idea. Supermoto was most popular in Europe for more than two decades. Then the **American Motorcycling Association (AMA)** started its Supermoto Championship in 2003. Supermoto has exploded in popularity in the United States since then.

Fast Fact

Supermoto is especially popular in France. There it is called "supermotard."

EQUIPMENT

Supermoto bikes are built to perform on both dirt and pavement. Most are **modified** motocross dirt bikes. The tires are smaller and smoother than typical dirt bike tires. Smooth tires have the best **traction** on paved surfaces. Small tires give the bike's rider more control. A strong **suspension system** helps supermoto bikes handle the rough dirt sections of a course. Supermoto bikes have big, powerful engines. These are built for quick bursts of speed.

Supermoto riders
need good safety gear.
Riders move in tight packs.
Crashes are common.
Helmets with face shields
are essential. Long leather
clothing, boots, and gloves
are important. Riders may
even wear **body armor**
beneath their clothing.

SUPERMOTO IN ACTION

Supermoto racing is a true challenge for motorcycle riders. Paved and dirt surfaces test riders in different ways. Most motorcycle riders today specialize in one surface or the other. Supermoto riders must master both.

The paved section features amazing speeds and bike handling skills. Riders can go as fast as 120 miles (193 kilometers) per hour or more on the long straightaways. Sharp turns require careful control of the bike. Riders have to lean hard toward the pavement while they turn.

The dirt section has its own challenges. Riders must know how to handle loose, slippery terrain. They must know how to land jumps. Often there are a series of small, tricky dirt jumps called **whoops**. Then there are one or more big jumps. The big jumps can send riders flying 10 feet (3 meters) or more in the air. Riders typically circle the entire course two or three times in one race.

A supermoto event includes several races. The first races are the **heats**. The top nine finishers in each of two heats advance to the final. The remaining riders race in the **last chance qualifier (LCQ)**. The top two finishers in the LCQ make it to the final. The final is the championship race. Only the fastest rider takes the **checkered flag**.

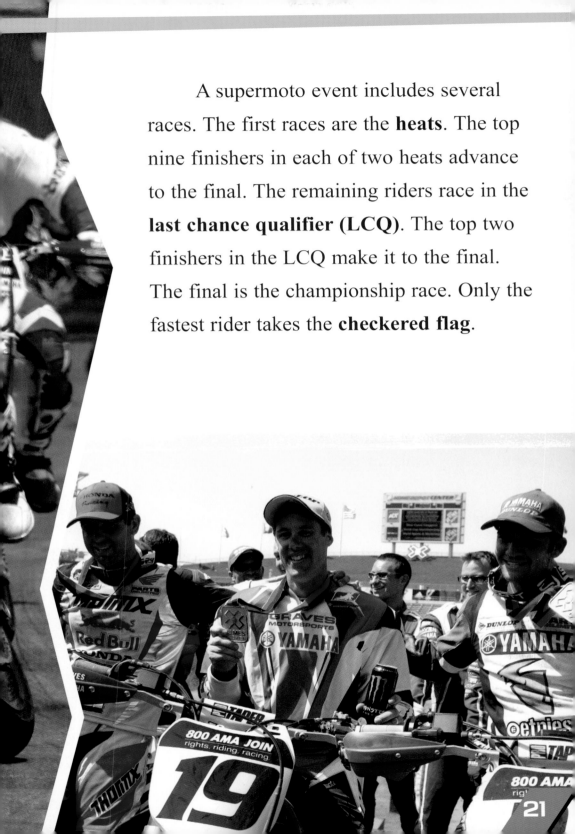

GLOSSARY

American Motorcyclist Association—a U.S. organization of more than 280,000 motorcyclists; the AMA organizes many motorcycling activities and events.

body armor—a strong, body-fitting piece of plastic and foam that supermoto riders wear underneath their clothes to protect them during crashes

checkered flag—the flag waved at the end of a race; the winner is said to "take the checkered flag."

heat—a qualifying race

last chance qualifier (LCQ)—a race in which those riders who failed to finish high enough in their heat get a second chance to qualify for the final

modify—to change; motocross racing bikes are modifed for supermoto.

motocross—a sport in which riders race motorcycles on outdoor dirt courses with lots of jumps and turns

road race—a motorcycle race held on flat, paved tracks

suspension system—the series of springs and shock absorbers that connect the body of a vehicle to its wheels

traction—the grip of the tires on a racing surface

whoops—a series of small jumps on a supermoto course

TO LEARN MORE

AT THE LIBRARY

Armentrout, David. *Motorcycle Races*. Vero Beach, Fla.: Rourke, 2008.

David, Jack. *Motocross Racing*. Minneapolis, Minn.: Bellwether, 2008.

Mezzanotte, Jim. *Supermoto*. Milwaukee, Wisc.: Gareth Stevens, 2006.

ON THE WEB

Learning more about supermoto is as easy as 1, 2, 3.

1. Go to www.factsurfer.com
2. Enter "supermoto" into search box.
3. Click the "Surf" button and you will see a list of related web sites.

With factsurfer.com, finding more information is just a click away.

INDEX

DATE DUE

DEMCO, INC. 38-2931